The Shore

A Collection of Reflective Poetry by a Lochaber Lass

Written by
Mabel MacRae Anderson

Dedication

This Collection of Poetry is dedicated to the memory of my brother, Robert MacRae, aged 19 years, who took a long walk on 7th February, 1975, never to return Home to his heartbroken family and friends:-

"For a Life that should have been,
Your memory forever green,
For you my brother, my trusted friend,
Until we meet on The Shore again."

Many thanks to Stuart Ross, Roy Bridge, for the cover photograph of Caol Shore, Loch Linnhe

Introduction

This Collection of poetry was inspired by my childhood, my family, my friends and my life experiences. A Highlander by blood and birth, I was born in the small West Highland village of Caol, nestled at the foot of Ben Nevis and by the shore of Loch Linnhe, in beautiful Lochaber. Here I grew up in a loving family, the youngest of five children and the only girl, which, of course, meant I was very protected and loved. Our family was part of a close knit community, where we nurtured each other and cared for our neighbours and friends. There was always a great sense of camaraderie. The poetry to a large extent, is auto biographical, relating thoughts, feelings and ultimately trying to make sense, make meaning of this Life, and of the Journey.

I have enjoyed writing throughout my life, but it wasn't until I started a Facebook page, Muse At Mabel, www.facebook.com/mabel.anderson.731, that I began to share what I had written with "the World". The poetry is about Love, Life, Death, Loss, Longing, Belonging, Home, Truth and most of all Healing, our Universal Experiences. I found that my poetry had great appeal and gained many readers on this Facebook page. From as far flung as my Home town, throughout the UK, and across the ocean to the USA, Canada and parts of Europe. This was quite astounding! I realised then that my poetry had Universal appeal, our Universal life experiences were written in every line and held meaning, bringing both release and healing to my readers. This gave me a true sense of purpose, and with the continuing encouragement and support of my Audience, I found that my writing was flowing, and ultimately led to the publication of this Collection of reflective poetry.

Thus, I thank you all from the bottom of my heart, dear friends, family and readers for helping me to find my true Path in Life, and I hope that I can continue to write for you, in a thought provoking, yet philosophical way, bringing love, peace and healing to all. If my poetry be the food of the Soul, Read On.................

Mabel MacRae Anderson
Muse At Mabel on Facebook
www.facebook.com/mabel.anderson.731

Caol Shore

From the Corpach basin, along Caol shore,
In the near distance, Ben Nevis soars,
A majestic giant, guardian of the Glen,
For countless years and lives of men,
Fair Loch Linnhe, the sapphire blue gem,
Tides flowing in and ebbing again,
An old boat lies, brought to rest,
On shingled shore, well past her best,
Taste of salt upon the lips,
Sea breeze blowing, water whips,
Crunching seaweed gives way to sand,
Turning tide gives way to land,
Overhead fast moving clouds,
A hint of moisture on the brow,
Looking backwards, shops and school,
Childhood home, the village of Caol,
Thoughts of family and of friends,
A pleasure to remember them,
Turning back toward the Loch,
A familiar and inspiring walk,
Pause for a moment, to drink it in,
This feeling - that I'm home again.

Un - Clearances

A Highlander by blood and birth,
By Nation, a Scot, from the North,
My mother tongue was lost to me,
The Gaelic language, a mystery,
When generations past, our culture was riven,
As from our homelands we were driven,
This hurt still heavy in our hearts,
These memories do not depart,
In our music and our song,
You'll hear the echoes of what is gone,
As with the flow and ebb of the sea,
The longing in my Poetry,
But like the sea, the tide is turning,
Culture resurges, time to stop mourning,
Those times long gone in history,
Be aware of new opportunity,
To own our land, to walk again,
Our Homes rebuilt by loch and glen,
At last the Circle turns full tilt,
Restoration of the Gaelic lilt.

Eilean Donan

Castle stands guard o'er the bay,
Eilean Donan, stronghold of MacRae,
Eternal waters stir memory,
Sagas told of days of glory,
Proud birlinns on a salty highway,
Lords of the Isles, a trusty byway,
MacNeils of Barra, MacLeans of Mull,
Proud masters of a sleek ship's hull,
No rule by a foreign power's hand,
A life, a culture, clan to clan,
Clan to clan, man to man,
Sea farers and skilled fisherman,
A mother tongue, the Gaelic lilt,
Music, art, once custom built,
Ruthlessly subdued and ethnically cleansed,
The Gael returns to sea again,
Highways restored, the Gael resurges,
And with a new will re-emerges,
A new tide sweeping in again,
That takes back lochan, sea and glen,
Reclaiming our heritage and our clan,
So whisper the echoes of Eilean Donan.

On the Road to Kinlochleven

On the old road to Kinlochleven,
Rise and fall, surface uneven,
Surrounded , enveloped in verdant splendour,
My soul uplifted, as I endeavour,
To traverse this road in front of me,
My hopes and dreams I clearly see,
Just like this road, it's dips and hills,
My mind with memories, is filled,
Of days that passed, the bad, the good,
Of Home and hearth, of Kin and blood,
How Life's Road itself, was rough, uneven,
Just like this road to Kinlochleven,
Yet all around was beauty and growth,
Surrounded by an emerald host,
I opened my eyes and drank it in,
Listening, as the leaves were rustling,
Moving forward through a dappled arch,
My soul was singing, I relished this march,
Being aware of the beauty surrounding me,
In plain sight for all to see,
Hope sprang in my heart, fresh and new,
For the wonder of this Life, for all I would do,
In that moment, my spirit was reborn again,
On the old, bumpy road to Kinlochleven.

Caledonian Canal

Crisp, cottony snow, crunching underfoot,
Somewhere in the half light, an owl hoot,
Horizon bathed in a haze of gold,
Over Loch Linnhe, as dreams unfold,
Caley Canal, Telford's triumphant deed,
A dream made real by a hardy breed,
Navvies, journeymen, master engineer,
Skill and endeavour, blood, sweat and tears,
This dream took shape, a thing of beauty,
As man, woman and child attended to duty,
So we may walk and sail, find pleasure,
In a landscape divine, yet man-made in it's measure,
A magical, mystical scene of serentity,
Contemplation, sensation of touching eternity,
A moonlit walk on the banks of this place,
A feeling of divinity, of nearness to grace,
Sun setting in pink and golden hues,
Over Loch Linnhe, where else would you choose?
To watch the sunset, or see it rise again,
Entwining Nature with the work of men,
Ben Nevis forever flows up from the sea,
Ever watchful of Glen Mhor, a faithful trustee,
A sacred landscape, it's beauty not frail,

Now and forever the Home of the Gael,
The place where I learned, loved and grew,
The people I respected, admired and knew,
Some no longer walk in this magical land,
Yet Spirit endures, as endless as sand,
The echoes of those who have come and gone,
Yet new footsteps are made by those who belong,
From the Caley Canal, to the Shore of Caol,
Sunset o'er Loch Linnhe, your soul will pull,
A glorious song of before, now and then,
Till you walk the canal banks and Caol Shore again.

I'm from Caol

Born in 1963, the President was John F Kennedy,
Went to school in '68, Caol Primary, it was great
Felt excited, Fiona was sad, I didn't know why,
There was quite a bit of howling and starting to cry.....
The football team, the choir, playing the chanter,
Playground games and lots of banter.

Sheila's mum made great chips,
Cath's mum supplied choccie biscuits.
Caroline's dad loved Shirley Bassey,
"Kiss me Honey," yes, what a classic!
Fiona's mum taught us how to use make up,
Life long friendships that would never break up.

Mairi and Rhona called every day,
To go to school, to find the way,
Times were hard then and I never really knew,
How much I relied on all of you.
We were bonded by birth, of the same creed,
There for each other in times of need.

Going to the chippy, taking the bus,
Cinema in Fort William was a must,
Zippers, trench coats, straight legged jeans
Must have the latest gear, by any means!
The Milton and Tavvies, days of glory,
We lived and carried on the age old story.

Riding hard on the motorbike
Fast cars and racing – what were we like!
Things started to change, some moved away,
Some got married, some stayed.........
So Years have passed, but we'll never forget,
And, most of all, there will be good times yet!

Life's True Companions

Friends who know you, through and through -
And who love you in spite of that!
Friends you know, are there for you,
Although you're miles apart,
Friends whose souls are destined to be,
Forever in each other's hearts,
These bonds of friendship last life long,
In an uncertain world - we can be sure of that.

Cath

A life long friendship is precious and rare,
I can't remember a time when you weren't there,
We were born within a stone's throw of each other,
We played, ran wild, we grew up together,
Our bond wasn't blood, but just as strong,
There is no doubt that it will be life long,
You're one of a kind, the best I've known,
Through thick and thin, our bond has grown,
I wish we saw each other more often than we do,
But you have commitments and I do too,
The nights we shared in the good old Town,
Strutting our stuff on the hallowed ground!
Always there for each other, had each other's back,
An ally, a confidante, we did not lack,
When times were dark, we both knew great sorrow,
But we gave each other hope, for a better tomorrow,
It's a bond that's there, it's meant to be,
Never difficult, always joyous, it's plain to see,
We've been blessed to know what true friendship is,
'Twill ever be so, as long as we live.

Mother

You gave me life, you raised me well,
You picked me up whenever I fell,
Your tender touch soothed a fevered brow,
You made everything better, as only you knew how,
Your curly dark hair, eyes of deepest blue,
Full of compassion for all that you knew,
Full of love and full of grace,
Set clear and true in your beautiful face,
Your smile could make the world seem bright,
Your burden was the darkest night,
You had the strength and courage to prove,
That life's sorrows would not embitter you,
Whenever I'm weak or feeling down,
I think of you and what you would have done,
Your capacity to love, your ability to give,
Most of all, your power to forgive,
I try my best to be true to you still,
I love you, honour you and I always will.

Embrace

Moments of quiet, moments of peace,
Take time to allow yourself release
From the hustle and bustle, rushing around,
In these moments, your soul can be found,
To see the world in all it's wonder,
Our very existence you may ponder,
The glory of nature, mountains and trees,
Loch Linnhe as she flows fulsome and free,
The Caley Canal, best of nautre and man,
Giving Glen Mhor a flowing span,
On a glorious and serene Winter morn,
Ben Nevis smiles, benevolent and strong,
Knowing possessions bring a fleeting high,
Worries and cares that make you sigh,
Are banished, at least for a while,
This land, our Home, our hearts doth beguile,
As walking these old familiar ways,
Reminds us of our own mortality,
What matters, what true, it's hard to say,
But you'll feel it in your soul when you walk today,
A glorious day, a bountiful life, time to banish any doubt,
Embrace it, take it and make it truly count.

The Long Goodbye

Lost in grief, impenetrable and deep,
For many a day I could not sleep,
I closed my eyes, twas late one night,
Within a heartbeat, my dreams took flight.
I saw your face, your eyes, your smile,
I held you close, we talked a while.
I told you how I missed you so
And did not understand why you had to go.
You said it was your time to pass,
The sand ran through the hour glass.
That each of us burns long or bright,
Until we disappear from sight.
You told me I must laugh and cry,
I should not let life pass me by,
That I must let go of the past,
And hold sweet memories in my heart.
There would be joys, there would sorrows
But most of all, there would be tomorrows.
I didn't want the dream to end,
It felt as though I was losing you again,
You gave me one last longed for smile,
I knew then, it would be a while,
Until we met and embraced again,
But that I would live and love till then.

I Miss You

I miss you.........
I knew I couldn't make you stay,
That there would be no other day,
This parting was an end forever,
No more lingering days together,
Those lovely eyes so blue and bright,
A smile to light the darkest night,
A touch that healed, a voice that soothed,
A compassionate heart, so easily moved,
I miss you...........
I would love to sit and talk with you,
Even for a mere minute or two,
To take your hand, hold you close,
To see your eyes, hear your voice,
Longing to tell you of my Life,
Longing to know that you're all right,
Longing to be with you again,
It may be a while, but until then,
I miss you............

Empty Space

Goodbye my brother, my trusted friend,
I never expected this sudden end,
I thought of all that we've been through,
The good, the bad, the hard times too,
It's heartbreaking to accept that what I'll see,
Is a "You" shaped space, where "You" used to be,
Instead of you sitting in a favoured chair,
Where, I'll look for you - you won't be there,
That we'll no longer share a laugh, a smile,
No more walks together on a golden mile,
Wishing we could have one last conversation,
Before reaching that final destination,
To be taken away without the chance,
For one last embrace, one last dance,
One last opportunity to say,
That I loved you so much, every day,
I hope you'll be waiting when I reach my end,
Goodbye my brother, my trusted friend.....

'Til Eternity

Torn away.............
On a bleak winter's day,
Too late now, to hope, or pray,
Grief so raw, cuts like a knife,
For the loss of such a precious life,
Father, son, husband, brother,
Irreplaceable. by any other,
Tears unending, silent grief,
Death comes uninvited, as a thief,
Memories will be honoured, eulogies spoken,
Gifts given in Life, forever a token,
No words or deeds can ever ease this pain,
But know that you will meet again,
On the shores of the eternal sea,
Taking your hand for eternity.

Silence

My silence holds a thousand thoughts,
Of, "ifs" and "buts", "what ifs", "why nots",
If only you were here with me,
But I know that can never be,
What if I could have held you close,
Why not a story to unfold?
If life was simple, true and free,
But this, it seems, can never be,
What if in some imagined land,
Why not your heart be in my hand?
My silence holds a thousand thoughts,
Of love and what my soul's been taught.

Longing - Belonging

You're far away........
From me today,
This distance between us, over land and sea,
Yet I feel you near,
See your eyes, so clear,
As I look into your soul, your thoughts I hear,
Thoughts and feelings, so divine,
My heart is yours, as yours is mine,
Feel my breath whisper upon your face,
"Soon, my Lover, we will embrace,"
Our passion knows no limit, or bounds,
As deep and true, this love that we've found,
Pure, a meeting of spirit and souls,
As our Fate decrees and Destiny unfolds,
The gap will be breached, will no longer be.......
When I lie in your arms, and you lie with me,
Yet, you're far away.......
From me today,
This distance between us, over land and sea.

Love Song

I wanted to write a Love Song..........
About the Moon and the Magic of the Night,
Of Star-crossed Lovers, whose Hearts take flight,
Of Passion so deep that the World fades away,
Of Loving and giving each and every day,
I know I can write a Love Song............
About the pain and the thrill of desire,
Of Forbidden Fruit, and Earthly mire,
Of the lows, as well as the highs,
Of how Love can burn, and sometimes die,
I'm going to write a Love Song............
About when I first laid eyes on you,
Our eyes locked together, blue on turquoise blue,
Our bodies entwined in pleasure so deep,
Our souls were mated, no longer asleep,
I really have to write a Love Song..........
About wanting to be with you,
Of a Fate, that seems to dictate, we're destined to be We two,
Of dancing minds and hearts that fly,
Of never letting Life pass us by,
I think this is Our Love Song............

Renewal

Our love is an old love,
Forged in the fire,
When we were young,
Full of passion and desire,
Many years pass,
Children are born,
Our time is divided,
Our loyalties torn,
We work hard
And often forget,
To make time for each other,
Our pleasures well met,
This time of renewal,
Is long overdue,
I pledge to you now,
Let's be ever true,
Renew our bonds and faith in each other,
My anchor, my rock, my best friend and lover.

Falling

I remember those deep brown eyes,
Smiling, as they drank me in,
I remember those deep brown eyes,
Voraciously, studying,
My eyes, my face, my form, my grace,
As you held me close in passionate embrace,
A dance of sensuous desire and love,
World disappears, no below or above,
Deep brown eyes locked on turquoise blue,
No questions asked, my soul you knew,
With those deep brown eyes, I knew no fear,
Only that I must have you here,
Falling forever into those deep brown eyes,
With love and pleasure and passionate sighs.

Sunday Best

Here we lie on Sunday morn',
Still abed, yet it's way past dawn,
A peaceful closeness, bound together,
Wishing to stay like this forever,
Old lovers, old friends, our story goes on,
Our journeys entwined, eternally strong,
Life can be sweet on a Sunday morn',
To savour, to relish, before it' s gone,
So here it is my Sunday best,
May today and every day be so blessed.

Promise

It's late........
Too late to say?
How sorry I am,
For being less than,
A trusted friend,
There till the End,
I'm only human,
Just a woman......,
Flawed, yet true,
Just like you....,
I didn't mean to cause you pain,
I know that you want to live again,
Release the hurt that runs so deep,
Cry those tears, you need to weep,
I've known you time and again,
Our souls entwined, fated, meant,
Let go of the past, have the power to forgive,
This is the Time, to love and live.

Grace

Breeze whispering through my window,
A taste of early dawn on my lips,
Dreamless sleep bringing deep healing
My body filled with grace and a glowing feeling,
A gentle awakening in the morning hush,
Enfolded, in the arms of the man I love,
Feeling at peace, all as it should be,
As the tides turn and the sun shines in the heavens above.

He Likes It

Fill my cup with your sweet love,
Of you, I'll never have enough,
You've loved me long, you've loved me true,
And I love just to be with you,
Although life sometimes brings us down,
I feel at peace when you're around,
You've sheltered me, picked me up,
Together we sipped from the Lover's Cup,
To be as one, to be together,
In past, in present and forever.

Protection

An Angel's breath upon my face,
I seek protection in your Grace,
Under siege, by demons of old,
Open wounds and hurts untold,
Enfold me in your gentle Wings,
I long for Healing to begin,
Help me to release this pain,
Heal me, make me whole again,
Rivers of tears, a blackened soul,
A broken spirit, blood will flow,
My Trust has been so vilified,
Sometimes I've wished that I would die,
I need you Angel, Mother, Protector,
Come to me, your Earth bound daughter,
Enfold me in your gentle Wings,
Heal me, make me live again.

The Blessing

Thoughts of the past, of family and friends,
Thoughts of the folk I won't see again,
Thoughts of days and nights and years,
Thoughts of when I held you near,
Knowing that those times have passed,
Knowing life is transient, not made to last,
Knowing that I've made many errors,
Knowing that I should have done better,
Wishing I could say I'm sorry,
Wishing I hadn't made you worry,
Wishing I could talk with you,
Wishing we could start anew,
Finding at last, it's easy to say,
Finding those words that were locked away,
Finding that it's easy to forgive,
Finding that it's good to live,
Thinking, I'll let go of the past,
Thinking, I'll live life while it lasts,
Thinking, it's here and now that counts,
Thinking, that this is what life is about,
Believing that today, I'll do my best,
Believing that life will put me to test,
Believing that life's true lesson,
Is believing, Life truly is The Blessing.

Seeing

Moving forward, moving on,
Doesn't mean I've forgotten what's gone,
Will honour the past, but live for today,
Be myself - knowing that's OK,
For all the highs, lows, joys and sorrows,
Make the most of today, and hope for tomorrows,
Lift the dark veil, open my eyes and see,
Appreciate the everyday beauty that surrounds me
In the eyes and the smile of a beloved one,
In the sea, the sky, the clouds and the sun,
Express my love, know that I'm loved too,
Realise potential, let your light shine through.

The Green Grass

Was walking the old ways,
Thinking of the old days,
Of Family, of Friends,
Of Beginnings, of Ends
Remembering the Fathers, the Mothers,
The sisters and the brothers,
What they were like then,
And the ones I won't see again.

Thought about my mother,
Always in a rush,
My father in his uniform,
Proud to drive the bus,
My four big brothers, never at a loss,
Who was best at what, and who would be the boss.
Thought about myself and my wee red bike,
Playing at Lupin Island, curly-haired wee tyke!

All the children we played with, but to name a few,
Kennedys, Donnellys, MacLeans, MacDonalds too
Caol was full of children
Like a great, big Zoo!

Never will forget those days,
They were the very best
Growing up together,
In our very own Wild West!

The teenage years brought dark, dark times,
Our family was broken and shattered,
Trying to make sense of it all
And figure out what mattered.
Wanted to thank you all my friends,
Would never have come through without you,
All those crazy drunken ceilidhs,
And the cars and motorbikes too!

Those days are long past now,
Although sometimes I can almost touch them,
And Loch Linnhe still shines
Like a sapphire blue gem.
Our childhood paths are never forgotten,
Long and winding and so well trodden,
My Family, Friends, Keepers of the soul,
We'll journey on together, new stories will unfold!

Consider the Bluebells

Bluebells on a sloping hill,
Swaying gracefully, never still,
A sea of flowers on the lochan's shore,
Bountifully giving at the church's door,
Heavy, musky, familiar scent,
Scotland's bluebells, heaven sent,
A tenacious flower, strong and true,
A symbol of our country too,
Consider the Blubells, Nature's treasure,
In how our National identity measures -
A beauty born of endurance to cold,
Of taking the chance to stand tall and bold,
A sign, a portent, Nature's blessing?
Our country's future, in assessing?
Take meaning from the Bluebells story,
Endure, stand tall, a triumphant glory,
This sea of blue and Scottish power,
Our Nation too, can reach full flower,
When we allow full vent to Spring,
And like the Bluebells dance and sing,
Our own Song, to our own beat,
Our country's Destiny to meet,
As bluebells dancing on the hill,
We can be our own Nation, and we will,

Have courage in our strength to endure,
Like Bluebells we will bloom once more,
Strong, independent, growing year after year,
Consider the Bluebells, our Spring time is here.

Horns

A hardy breed, a handsome beast,
A finer animal, you'll never meet,
Burnished copper, countenance strong,
Fearsome horns, curved and long,
Just like the Gael, somewhat rare,
Just like the Gael, he's still there,
A beloved emblem of the past,
Tough and tenacious, made to last,
Patiently waiting, no more to roam,
Patiently waiting, to reclaim our Home,
Lands of the Gael, grass is so sweet,
Clinging tenaciously, man and beast meet,
A future long waited for, when once again,
The Gael and the beast return to the Glen.

Surrounded

Wishing for your heart to heal,
With pain so deep, you've had to deal,
Knowing that you'll hurt forever,
Knowing you have the spirit to weather,
The dark days that consumed your life,
To the beautiful times, that are filled with light,
An angel watches over you,
To love and support you, and help you through,
Surrounded with love and a blessing to give,
Peace and healing, to go forward and live.

Creativity

Someone very dear to me,
Asked me about my poetry,
"Do you even know where it comes from?
This urge to write, that is so strong,"
I couldn't answer him there and then,
I had wanted to write since way back when,
It was something inside, soulful and pure,
A way of releasing the pain I'd endured,
Give meaning and voice to experience of life,
A process of revealing both triumph and strife,
They say "the poet needs the pain,"
Yet the poetry healed me and let me live again,
When life"s sorrows hurt us, we shut the world out,
Consumed by the burden of pain and doubt,
Why must this happen? Why is this so?
Does anybody care? Why did you go?
My soul and my spirit were crippled with pain,
This is when I realised that it's not all in vain,

If you have a gift, be it poetry, music or art,
The ability to give and open your heart,
Share your gift, cherish this opportunity to live,
Use your powers to love and to forgive,
There's this one life, we don't know for how long,
So make the most of our gifts, be it poetry, art or song.

Touching Eternity

From atop the highest mountain, a Canvas of Creation stretched in front of Me and surrounded Me;
I knew then, that I had but to stretch forth my Hand to touch Eternity.......
Cloth of midnight blue enlightened by a spray of silver stars andan enchanted Moon,
Dark yielding to light, weaving shades of grey, grey blue and pink
As a golden Sun ascends, son of Heaven, illuminating, creating Life,
Sowing seeds, our fertile Mother, brings forth her bountiful beauty,
This mountain where I stand, her vista to an endless ocean,
Deep, divine water, giving Life and from which Life emerges,
Verdant hills and valleys, trees stand tall and deep rooted in fertile soil,
Meadows of sweet scented blooms, a riot of red, orange, gold and yellow,
Trees laden with citrus delights, figs and sumptious apples,

Ever a temptation to gorge ourselves on the other's gifts,
Take in, devour her friuts, so freely given up for our nourishment and pleasure,
This canvas, this glorious Creation, we should revere, we must reciprocate,
With care, with Love, not just take, but give back and know true Enlightenment,
I know now, that I have but to stretch forth my Hand, to touch Eternity.........

Sleepwalking

On a clear, cool, crisp Winter's eve,
From a roaring fire, we take our leave,
To take a walk on the Shore at Caol,
Down past the shops and the primary school,
Emerging onto a shingly beach,
Seaweed and sand underfeet,
Air is cool, refreshing, moonlight,
Feel the enchantment of the night,
At our heels, our faithful friend,
Alert, his territory to defend,
His nose sees more than we can know,
As to the lochside we go,
Waves are lapping on the Shore,
Tide's coming in, encroaching more,
The base around the tethered boat,
Becomes submerged and begins to float,
Mysterious night, the senses sharpen,
As clouds obscure the Moon, it darkens,
In the distance the lights of Town,
Their reach extends across and down,
Lightly illuminating the Shore at Caol,
Welcoming, beckoning, they have a pull,
Alluring, this beauty of the night,
Although it partly obscures the sight,

Yet still the looming shadow of the Ben,
Assures me that I'm home again,
Memories of my family, my folk,
Memories of the words we spoke,
I waken with a start and then,
Realise I've had this dream again.

Return of The Gael

Red, yellow flowers, a distant blue,
Set within a verdant hue,
Scented sweetly, on sea breeze,
Enhancing, dancing, feeling of ease,
Wild flowers on the Machair grass,
Give way to silver sands at last,
Moist and cottony underfoot,
Socks are off, removing boots!
Oyster catchers on the beach,
Long red bills, chirping, "kleep, kleep,"
Wind whips hair upon my face,
Catching me in lively embrace,
Scanning seawards, a boat perhaps,
A birlinn, galley from the Past?
Echoes of a time long gone,
When Gaels once sang another Song,
Speaking in our mother tongue,
Our land our own, no need to run,
These oceans took our blood away,
A longing to return one day,
Alight upon the silver sands,
To tread once more the Machair lands.

Printed in Great Britain
by Amazon